The Holy Mass
Coloring and Activity Book

Together We Celebrate the Eucharist!

Written by
Ancilla Christine Hirsch, FSP

Illustrated by
Virginia Helen Richards, FSP

Pauline
BOOKS & MEDIA

Nihil Obstat:
Rev. Alfred McBride, O.Praem, Ph.D.

Imprimatur:
+Bernard Cardinal Law
February 12, 2002

Printed and published in the U.S.A. by Pauline Books & Media, 50 Saint Pauls Avenue, Boston, MA 02130-3491.

www.pauline.org

Pauline Books & Media is the publishing house of the Daughters of St. Paul, an international congregation of women religious serving the Church with the communications media.

2 3 4 5 6 7   08 07 06 05 04 03

Let's Get Ready!

Sunday is a special day when we celebrate God's greatest gift to us: Jesus. Jesus loves us so much that he died on the cross and rose from the dead for us. He is alive! On Sunday we go to church together. We thank God for all the gifts we receive every day.

Welcome!

We come to church to celebrate because we are God's family.
Let us love one another! Let us also come to church to hear God's Word
and to show our love and thanks and adoration to God, Father, Son and
Holy Spirit for his gifts to us.

Gathering Together at God's Table

We greet each other as we gather around the table of the Lord
to celebrate all that Jesus does for us. We remember the meal Jesus
shared with his apostles. We are ready to share this meal, too.

Come with Joy!

When we sing together we are all united as the Body of Christ.
We rejoice to be in the house of God and to be God's family.
We are ready to hear God's Word and celebrate the Eucharist.

Let's Begin

Father invites us to pray: **"In the name of the Father, and of the Son and of the Holy Spirit."** We pause to remember how God forgives us whenever we do not live according to God's ways. Lord, have mercy! We love you and want to live as you teach us!

You are the most high!

Glory to God!

On Sundays and special days we sing a song the Church has sung for many, many years: **Glory to God!** Peace to everyone!
God, we want to honor you and love you always.

Let us pray...

We bow our heads and pray to God.
After a few moments of silence, Father offers a prayer in the name of all
of us. We answer: **Amen!**

The Word of God

We listen to God's Word in the First Reading. We respond to this Word with the Responsorial Psalm. Then we hear the Second Reading.
God is speaking to us in these readings from the Bible. We listen carefully. We let God's Word reach into our hearts.

The Gospel of the Lord

We stand to listen to the very special words of the Gospel. We sing as
the Gospel book is carried high. The Gospel is the Good News of Jesus.
We want to hear Jesus' words to us. We pay attention.

The Homily

Father explains God's Word to us. He helps us to understand the
Readings and the Gospel. We learn how to live the way God wants us to.

The Profession of Faith

We believe! Together we declare what we
believe about God when we pray
the Nicene Creed. Many Christians
were killed as martyrs because
they believed these truths about God.
We are grateful to believe in God
and to share what we believe
with other people.

Lord, hear our prayer.

General Intercessions

Let us pray for the Church, for leaders, for all people, for those who are suffering, for all who have died. Lord, hear our prayer! We know you will take care of our needs.

Our Gift for the Church and the Poor

We want to share what we have and help people who have less than
we do. We do this by giving some of our money as a gift. Our gift also
supports the church, where we celebrate God's goodness to us. We put
our gift in the basket.

We Bring Our Gifts

Now some persons, who act for
everyone present, bring our
gifts of bread and wine to the
altar. God will take these gifts
and make them into
something new—the Body
and Blood of Jesus Christ!

The Preparation of the Gifts

We offer our gifts to God: Blessed be God forever! We join the angels and saints to sing: **"Holy, holy, holy Lord! Heaven and earth are full of your glory!"**

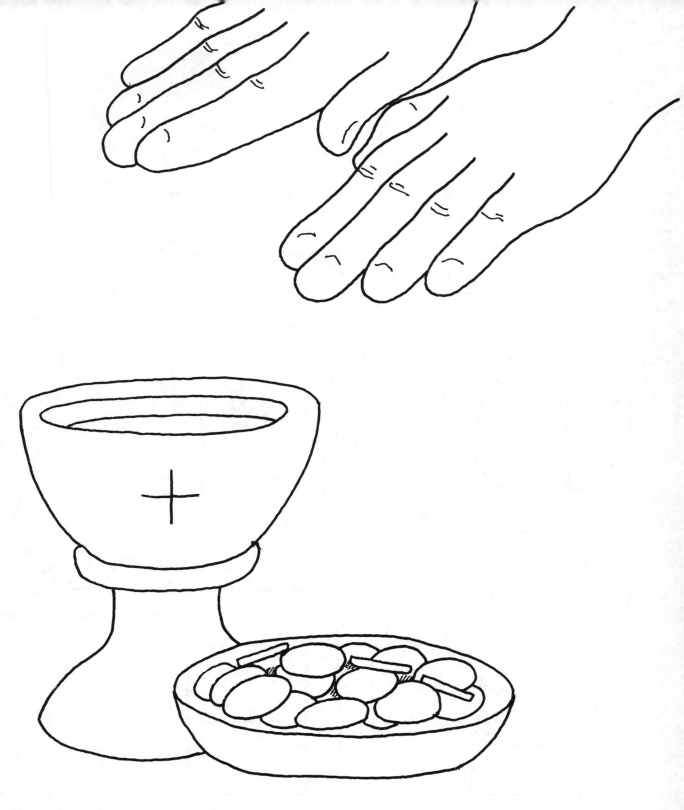

The Eucharistic Prayer

Father prays in the name of the whole Church, asking God's Spirit to come upon our gifts. We silently listen and pray: God our Father, accept this bread and wine as our offering. Accept us as an offering, too!

18

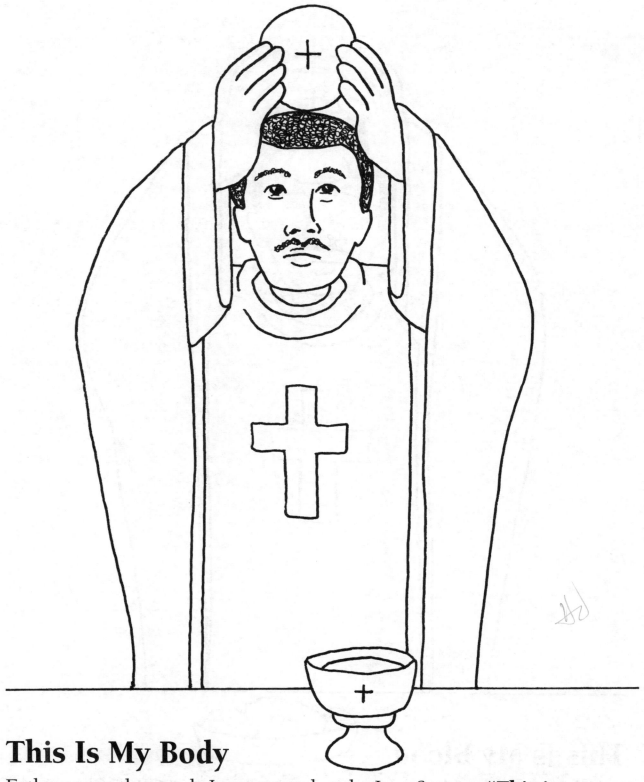

This Is My Body

Father prays the words Jesus prayed at the Last Supper: **"This is my body."** He lifts the bread so we can all see. Even though it still looks and tastes like bread, the bread is now the Body of Jesus! What a great gift! Jesus gave his body to death as a sacrifice on the cross so that all our sins could be forgiven.

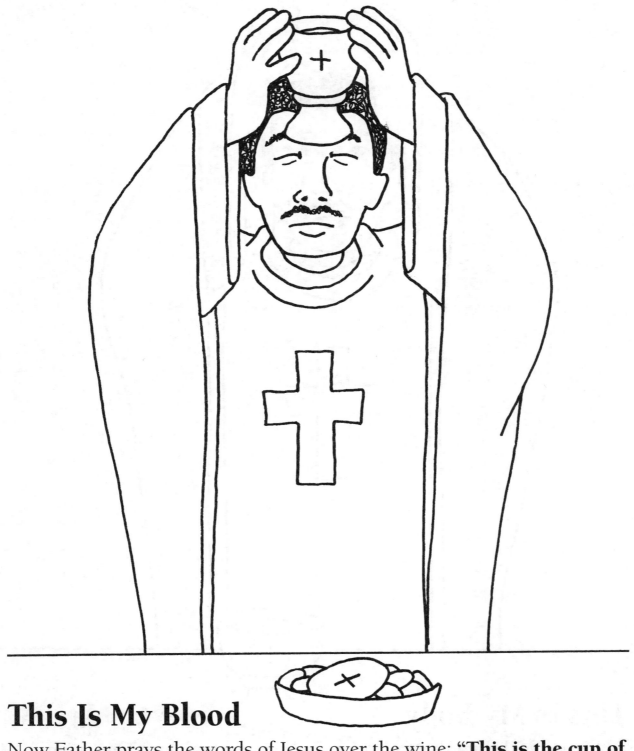

This Is My Blood

Now Father prays the words of Jesus over the wine: **"This is the cup of my blood."** Even though it still looks and tastes like wine, the wine is now the Blood of Jesus! Jesus poured out his blood as a sacrifice for the forgiveness of our sins because he loved us. We pray: Christ has died. Christ is risen. Lord Jesus, come in glory!

The Great Amen

At the end of this special prayer, Father holds the Eucharist, the Body and Blood of Jesus, above the altar. He prays in words like these:

"Through Christ, in him, with him—all glory and honor to God!"

We join our hearts to the whole prayer and sing: "Amen!" Yes!

The Lord's Prayer

Jesus taught us to pray: **"Our Father, who art in heaven…."**
Together we pray as God's children.

Peace be with you!
Peace be with you!

The Sign of Peace

Before we receive Jesus in the Eucharist, we want to be at peace with one another. We forgive those who have hurt us. We want to love as Jesus loves us. Peace be with everyone!

The Breaking of the Bread

The priest breaks the Bread of the Eucharist so that we can all receive the Body of Christ. **Lamb of God, you take away our sins. Have mercy on us.** Give us your peace and prepare our hearts to welcome you.

The Body of Christ

We receive Jesus in Holy Communion. We know this is the Body of Christ. Dear God, help us to become more like Jesus. Help us to be the Body of Christ.

The Blood of Christ

We may also receive the Blood of Christ in the Eucharist. Jesus loves us so much that he was willing to give his blood for us on the cross. Jesus, help us to do our best and to be generous with all people, just like you.

The Blessing

We pray for God's blessing on all of us and on the whole world. God, help us to live the joy that we have celebrated as your family. Send us into the world to witness to your love. We go out in peace to love and serve our God. **Thanks be to God!**

Living the Eucharist

When we celebrate the Eucharist or Mass together, we are made strong and are able to bring the love of God into our home, our school and our world. Let's love and serve each other as Jesus loves and serves us. Now we are the living Body of Christ. How can I be more loving?

Special Things Used at Mass

Draw a line from the words to each picture. Then color the pictures.

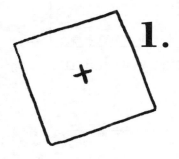 **1.**

 **2.**

 **3.**

 **4.**

 **5.**

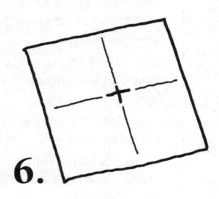 **6.**

a. The cup used for the wine is called a **chalice.** This cup is very special. We only use it at the Eucharist for the Blood of Jesus.

b. The **flagon** is a special pitcher used to hold more wine so that everyone will be able to receive the Blood of Jesus.

c. The **pall** is a small linen square that is made out of stiff material. It is used to cover the chalice.

d. The **purificator** is the linen cloth that is used to clean and dry the chalice.

e. The special plate for the bread is called a **paten.** This plate is used only to hold the Body of Jesus.

f. The **corporal** is a square piece of material that is laid on the altar under the chalice and paten.

answers:

What the Priest Wears at Mass

Word Box:

cincture	alb
chasuble	stole

Unscramble the words beside each picture. The new words you learn are also in the **Word Box.**

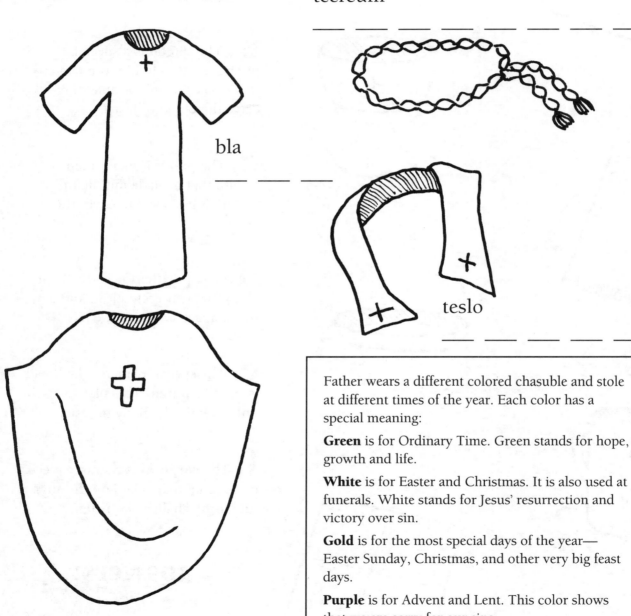

tccreuin

_ _ _ _ _ _ _ _

bla

_ _ _

teslo

_ _ _ _ _

hasculbe

_ _ _ _ _ _ _ _

Father wears a different colored chasuble and stole at different times of the year. Each color has a special meaning:

Green is for Ordinary Time. Green stands for hope, growth and life.

White is for Easter and Christmas. It is also used at funerals. White stands for Jesus' resurrection and victory over sin.

Gold is for the most special days of the year—Easter Sunday, Christmas, and other very big feast days.

Purple is for Advent and Lent. This color shows that we are sorry for our sins.

Red stands for the Holy Spirit, the blood of Jesus, and the blood of the martyrs. It's used on Pentecost and feasts that have to do with the cross of Jesus and the martyrs who died for Jesus.

It's Sunday!

Help Eric and his Mom find their way to the church for Mass.

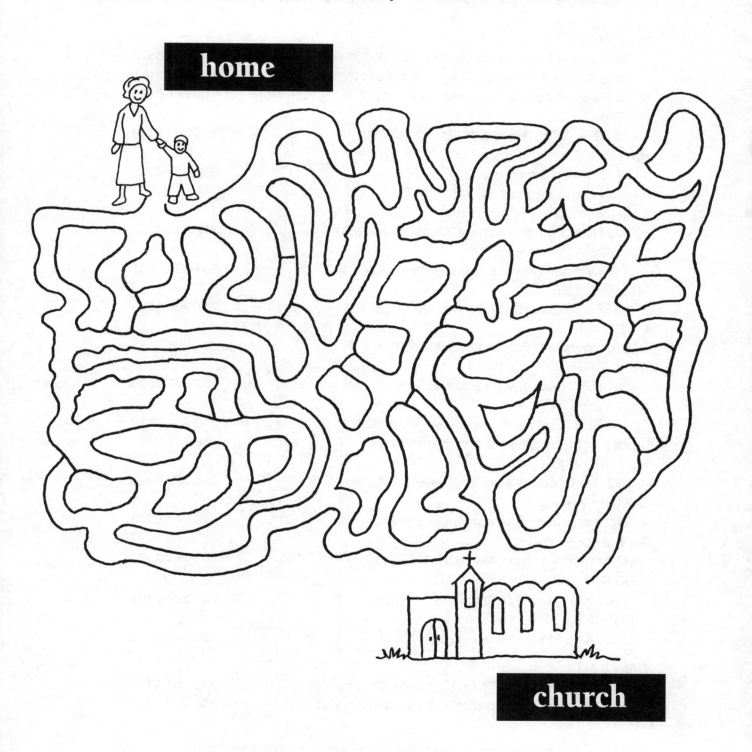

home

church

Pauline
BOOKS & MEDIA

The Daughters of St. Paul operate book and media centers at the following addresses. Visit, call or write the one nearest you today, or find us on the World Wide Web, www.pauline.org

CALIFORNIA
3908 Sepulveda Blvd, Culver City, CA 90230 — 310-397-8676
5945 Balboa Avenue, San Diego, CA 92111 — 858-565-9181
46 Geary Street, San Francisco, CA 94108 — 415-781-5180

FLORIDA
145 S.W. 107th Avenue, Miami, FL 33174 — 305-559-6715

HAWAII
1143 Bishop Street, Honolulu, HI 96813 — 808-521-2731
Neighbor Islands call: 800-259-8463

ILLINOIS
172 North Michigan Avenue, Chicago, IL 60601 — 312-346-4228

LOUISIANA
4403 Veterans Memorial Blvd, Metairie, LA 70006 — 504-887-7631

MASSACHUSETTS
885 Providence Hwy, Dedham, MA 02026 — 781-326-5385

MISSOURI
9804 Watson Road, St. Louis, MO 63126 — 314-965-3512

NEW JERSEY
561 U.S. Route 1, Wick Plaza, Edison, NJ 08817 — 732-572-1200

NEW YORK
150 East 52nd Street, New York, NY 10022 — 212-754-1110
78 Fort Place, Staten Island, NY 10301 — 718-447-5071

PENNSYLVANIA
9171-A Roosevelt Blvd, Philadelphia, PA 19114 — 215-676-9494

SOUTH CAROLINA
243 King Street, Charleston, SC 29401 — 843-577-0175

TENNESSEE
4811 Poplar Avenue, Memphis, TN 38117 — 901-761-2987

TEXAS
114 Main Plaza, San Antonio, TX 78205 — 210-224-8101

VIRGINIA
1025 King Street, Alexandria, VA 22314 — 703-549-3806

CANADA
3022 Dufferin Street, Toronto, Ontario, Canada M6B 3T5 — 416-781-9131
1155 Yonge Street, Toronto, Ontario, Canada M4T 1W2 — 416-934-3440

¡También somos su fuente para libros, videos y música en español!